T0353177

NATALIE MITCHELL

Natalie Mitchell writes for television, theatre and radio. She is currently writing a ten-part podcast drama for BBC Sounds alongside co-writer Vickie Donoghue. She was the only writer named on the Edinburgh TV Festival's Ones to Watch 2019 scheme and was named on the BBC Talent Hot List 2017.

Her theatre work includes *To My Younger Self* (Synergy Theatre); *Can't Stand Me Now* as part of the Royal Court Young Writers' Festival; *Crawling in the Dark* (Almeida Theatre); *When They Go Low* (National Theatre Connections); and *Germ Free Adolescent* and *This Wounded Island*, both of which were created with and for non-traditional theatre audiences in Kent. She has also had plays presented at Soho, Hampstead and Finborough Theatres.

TV includes episodes of *Holby City*, *Doctors*, *Ackley Bridge* and several years as a core writer on *EastEnders*. Radio includes *Proud* for BBC Radio 3 and *The Man Who Sold the World* and *Hidden Harm* for BBC Radio 4.

Natalie Mitchell

WHEN THEY GO LOW

NICK HERN BOOKS

London

www.nickhernbooks.co.uk

A Nick Hern Book

When They Go Low first published in Great Britain in 2020 as a paperback original by Nick Hern Books Limited, The Glasshouse, 49a Goldhawk Road, London W12 8QP

When They Go Low copyright © 2020 Natalie Mitchell

Natalie Mitchell has asserted her right to be identified as the author of this work

Cover image © Shutterstock.com/LightField Studios

Designed and typeset by Nick Hern Books, London
Printed in Great Britain by Mimeo Ltd, Huntingdon, Cambridgeshire PE29 6XX

ISBN 978 1 84842 902 4

A CIP catalogue record for this book is available from the British Library

Woodland
CARBON
www.woodlandcarbon.co.uk
NICK HERN BOOKS
Printed on Carbon Captured paper

When They Go Low was commissioned as part of the 2018 National Theatre Connections Festival and premiered by youth theatres across the UK, including a performance at the National Theatre in June 2018.

Each year the National Theatre asks ten writers to create new plays to be performed by young theatre companies all over the country. From Scotland to Cornwall and Northern Ireland to Norfolk, Connections celebrates great new writing for the stage – and the energy, commitment and talent of young theatremakers.

www.nationaltheatre.org.uk/connections

Acknowledgements

Thank you to everyone who contributed to the development of this play: the incredible NT Connections team; Tom Lyons for his dramaturgy; my amazing R&D facilitators Laura Keefe, Ros Terry and Jane Fallowfield; and particularly the young people who threw themselves into some difficult conversations and really helped to shape the play: St Saviours and St Olaves School, Brockhill School, City and Islington College, Gulbenkian Youth Theatre and Theatre Royal Stratford East Youth Theatre.

Author's Note

The chorus represents the wider world and community of the play, but exists in a slightly different universe – a liminal space separate from the naturalism of scenes between named characters. This may be online, or an alternate reality where they are looking in on the action. Lines are not attributed to specific individuals. There could be four of them, or forty. They should remain onstage the whole time, reacting, responding and taking on roles in scenes before melting back into the group. The only characters who should never also be part of the chorus are LOUISE, SCOTT, RACHEL, SHABS and CALEB.

Pacing is important. The play works best when it's fluid and fast-moving, with scenes crossing and blending in to each other, as the action our characters have set in motion begins to spiral out of their control.

N.M.

Characters

LOUISE
RACHEL
SHABS
SCOTT
CALEB
JADEN
CHARLIE
SARAH
MISS REEF
EMMELINE
HILLARY
MICHELLE
CHIMAMANDA
MADONNA
CHORUS

1.

– 'Two households, both alike in dignity – '

– Uh –

– That's the wrong –

– (*Raps the first two lines of the theme song to* The Fresh Prince of Bel Air.)

– Stop!

– That's not right either.

– What are you doing?

– Being the chorus.

– Introducing the story.

– That's what a chorus does, right?

– I think so.

– Yeah but –

– Not just that.

– They comment on it too.

– Introduce themes.

– React to things that happen.

– Represent the wider world of the play.

– I should've paid more attention in English.

– So what was the problem with –

– Well neither of those is our story.

– What is our story?

– Our story starts on an ordinary Saturday in September.

– Oh!

– That?

– Yeah.

– I actually think it started before then.

– Like when?

– Like, hundreds of years ago.

– I know what you're getting at, but I'm talking about this particular story.

– Our story.

– Which should be seen in the context of something bigger.

– Why?

– Because –

– Because?

– Well.

– This might be our story, but it could be other people's story too.

– You mean –

– It could have happened to other people.

– Doubt it.

– Maybe not exactly the same –

– But similar, maybe.

– So seeing all the little stories together as something bigger, it helps us –

– Understand.

– Why certain things happen.

– And maybe how to stop them happening again.

– S'pose.

– Okay.

– So –

– This is our story.

    A shift as the 'play' begins.

– Did you –

– Did you?

– What?

– Hear about Sarah.

– Sarah with the big –

– Yeah.

– No.

– What?

– Are you talking about –

– Blake's party?

– Was that good by the way?

– It was alright.

– It was amazing.

– Everyone was there.

– Even Smelly Anna.

– She got invited?

– I think her mum and Blake's mum are old friends.

– He didn't have a choice.

– That makes sense.

– Were you there?

– I didn't see you.

– I… couldn't make it. Busy.

– Not everyone then.

– That's a shame.

– You missed out.

– Did I though?

– Yeah.

– I heard Scott didn't make it either –

– He was there.

– Was he?

– Course.

– Charlie's brother, Scott?

– Yeah.

– Captain of the football team, straight As, fit as fuuu–

– Yeah. That Scott.

– Not a party without him.

– Is that why yours was so rubbish last year?

– Oooh!

– Burn.

– I thought you said you'd had a good time.

– I'm winding you up.

– And it worked.

– Yeah, well.

   Beat.

– So what happened then?

– Not much.

– Usual.

– Michael threw up in Sasha's mouth.

– That's disgusting.

– How's that even possible?

– Well, he started to, you know, heave.

– That was a rhetorical question.

– I meant what happened to Sarah.

– Dunno.

– You said –

– Oh yeah!

– Didn't she pass out?

– Such a lightweight.

– You must be talking about the picture.

– What picture?

– You didn't see it?

– No.

– The one she sent to –

– That wasn't her.

– Sounds like something she'd do.

– That definitely, a hundred per cent wasn't her.

– How do you know?

– I just do alright.

– Wasn't she kissing –

– Yeah!

– I heard that.

– I saw that.

– I heard it was more than that.

– No!

– Really?

– At the actual party?

– Yep.

– In Blake's bed.

– That's rotten.

– Unless it was with Blake.

– It wasn't.

– He was trying to pull Louise.

– Louise?

– Are you sure?

– Yep.

– But she's –

– I know.

– Blake was the one who found them, wasn't he?

– Them?

– Sarah was with more than one guy?

– Was she?

– I dunno. Was she?

– I dunno.

– Maybe.

– Probably.

– Definitely.

– So Sarah was with three blokes in Blake's bedroom.

– Receipts or it didn't happen.

– There's a photo isn't there.

– That's what we're talking about!

– You said there wasn't a photo.

– There isn't.

– There's a video.

– What!

– No way.

– Have you seen it?

– Course.

– It was online.

– Who put it there?

– Not sure.

– You didn't miss much.

– You watched it?

– I only saw the picture.

– I thought you said there was no picture?

– I'm confused.

– Don't be.

– I'm gonna look for it now.

– Then you can see.

– Any luck?

– Looks like it's been deleted.

– Maybe it never existed.

– It did.

– It was quite dark though.

– So it might not have been her.

– Oh it was definitely her.

– But it might not have been three?

– Could it've been more?

– Maybe.

– What!

– Sarah slept with four blokes in one night?

– I didn't say that.

– You literally just said –

– Not that she slept with any of them.

– She definitely didn't sleep with any of them.

– She's a virgin.

– Sarah?

– Steve said she's really frigid.

– Must be another Sarah.

– Guys.

– Maybe we shouldn't be talking about this.

– Why not?

– Everyone else is.

– And knowing Sarah –

– It's probably true!

– Yeah.

– I reckon it is.

– Me too.

– I just can't believe she'd sleep with four boys –

– Did she though?

– Yes!

– Has anyone bothered to ask?

– Or are you all too busy slut-shaming her?

2.

LOUISE, SCOTT, CALEB, RACHEL, SHABS, JADEN *and others waiting for their classroom to be unlocked.*

LOUISE. Is he still looking?

SHABS. If his eyes were laser beams. You'd be dead.

RACHEL. Just ignore him.

LOUISE. I still don't get what his problem is.

RACHEL. He's jealous you got a better grade than him.

LOUISE. That's not my fault, is it?

SHABS. In his head. Yes.

SCOTT. She is so smug.

JADEN. I know, right. Wait, what does smug mean?

SCOTT. I wouldn't be surprised if she only got an A cos she flirted with Mr Roberts.

JADEN. I've definitely seen her do that. Fluttering her eyelashes. It's so embarrassing.

CALEB. Why do you care what she got?

SCOTT. Because if she hadn't asked to change groups, we'd have got the same.

CALEB. B's still good.

SCOTT. Not when it's worth twenty per cent of your final grade and you need an A for your conditional offer.

JADEN. You gonna appeal?

SCOTT. Already have.

CALEB. I don't think one B is gonna make a difference. Not with all the other stuff you've got going for you.

SCOTT. Yeah well I can't take that risk. My dad's already fuming about how bad the football team's doing. 'Never lost a match under Charlie, did they?' If my grades drop too I dunno what he'll do.

A murmur goes through the crowd and people start walking away from the locked door.

LOUISE. What's going on? Mr Roberts isn't off again, is he?

STUDENT. All morning lessons cancelled. Special assembly for the girls.

RACHEL. For the girls?

As everyone heads off, SCOTT *and* LOUISE *come briefly face to face.*

LOUISE. Alright.

SCOTT. Alright.

LOUISE. Know what this is about?

SCOTT. Don't you?

LOUISE. No. That's why I'm asking.

JADEN. Who cares. We get a morning off timetable!

JORDAN *whoops and rushes off, followed by* SCOTT *and* CALEB. *The* GIRLS *remain.*

SHABS. Uh. It's obvious, isn't it.

LOUISE. No.

SHABS. It's the 'sex chat'.

RACHEL. You think?

SHABS. What else would it be?

3.

The girl's 'special' assembly.

MISS REEF. Now, today we have been made aware that there are some… unpleasant images circulating around the school.

RACHEL. Is she talking about Sarah?

SHABS. Blatantly.

LOUISE. Shh. She's right behind us.

MISS REEF. Whilst the incident in question did not happen on school property, we felt it appropriate to remind you girls how important it is to always… to always have self-respect.

LOUISE. What does that mean?

Er, miss –

MISS REEF. There'll be time for questions at the end, Louise.

What I mean is… well… Always think about what your behaviour and appearance says about you. Does it say, 'I am a respectable, intelligent young woman' or does it say… does it say… something else?

LOUISE. Miss?

MISS REEF. I said there'll be time at the end –

LOUISE. Are the boys gonna get the same lecture?

MISS REEF. This isn't a lecture.

LOUISE. Yes it is.

MISS REEF. You are always representing this school. And it's important you remember that responsibility. Just as we have a responsibility to help keep you safe. But fundamentally, we can't help you if it's your own behaviour that has put you at risk.

Beat. SARAH *rushes out of the assembly.*

RACHEL. Poor thing.

LOUISE. Oh Bondage! Up Yours!

'Oh Bondage! Up Yours!' by X-Ray Spex begins. A microphone drops down from the ceiling and the stage explodes with light and movement as the whole cast fill it. LOUISE *leads the company in a performance of the song, aimed at* MISS REEF. *Potentially, by the end of it,* MISS REEF *herself has taken over the lead vocals. When the song stops, everyone snaps back to exactly where they were before it started.*

MISS REEF. Louise? Did you have a question?

Beat.

LOUISE. No, Miss Reef.

The GIRLS *file out of assembly.* LOUISE *is furious.*

Do you know what that is? What that stupid… What she just did?

SHABS. Alright, soapbox, chill out.

RACHEL. She was just telling us to be sensible.

LOUISE. That is victim-blaming. Suggesting that Sarah deserved to, to be demeaned.

RACHEL. I don't think that is what she was saying.

SHABS. To be fair, none of this would've happened if Sarah hadn't been in a room with four blokes or whatever.

LOUISE. Oh my god. Don't you dare!

SHABS. What?

RACHEL. We don't know there were four.

LOUISE. That's not the point! The point is, she's getting hassled for something that wasn't her fault, when actually, those idiots should be punished.

SHABS. Punished for what though?

LOUISE. Are you winding me up?

SHABS. No. It's a serious question.

RACHEL. Shabs…

SHABS. What?

LOUISE. She passed out, they drew all over her, took pictures of it and then let people think she'd slept with them all, when she didn't. How is that alright?

I'm gonna go see Miss Reef. They should be suspended.

SHABS. Really?

LOUISE. Yeah. Yeah! Look. They didn't do it to be funny. They deliberately took advantage of someone and then publicly humiliated her, hiding behind the 'it was a joke' defence. And now she's the one being blamed for it!

SHABS. Is it really your business though?

LOUISE. Did you see her face in that assembly? She's got no one sticking up for her.

And that's… It's not fair.

Beat.

RACHEL. Every morning walking to school, there's this boy. Year 11 I think. Don't know his name. And he whistles at me when I pass. Then he tells me I have a nice arse. And I'm kind of… well you know how I feel about my… So I'm kind of flattered. But cos I don't reply he's started getting a bit, I dunno. Rude. Telling me I'm stuck-up. Fat. Stuff like that.

Beat.

And it's totally fine. Cos I just ignore him. But I suppose – I do kind of get what you're saying.

SHABS. I don't.

RACHEL. Well. It's that… maybe – maybe there are other people who'd like to, I dunno. Have someone to… Give them a voice. Stick up for them.

SHABS. Cos they don't have the guts to do it themselves.

RACHEL. Confidence, Shabs. And not everyone's got it by the bucketload like you do.

SHABS. Okay. So you get them suspended. Then what?

RACHEL. Well… I was kind of thinking maybe Louise should run for school captain.

– It was so awkward!

– Did you see her face?

– She was bright red.

– Staring at the floor.

– Hoping it would swallow her up.

– Do you think they should've talked to her alone?

– Maybe they did?

– To be fair they needed to say that.

– She should never have let herself be put in that position in the first place.

– I suppose not.

– So you think she was –

– Asking for it?

– Totally.

– If you're gonna get that drunk, you've got to expect someone to take the mick.

– Like you've never been that drunk.

– That happened once!

– Where were Stacey and Michelle?

– Shouldn't they have been looking out for her?

– Er, she's old enough not to need a babysitter.

– Did I hear right they've been suspended?

– What!

– Yeah

– Apparently.

– For how long?

– Dunno.

– I don't believe it.

– Was it her?

– Did she grass them up?

– Must've done.

– Does she know how much that could affect them!

– They're gonna miss mocks, aren't they?

– Yup.

– How could she do that to them?

– Over a joke.

– Hey.

– Hey!

– Sarah.

– Sarah.

– Sarah.

– Can't believe what a skank you are.

– Hashtag-drunk hashtag-Sarah-is-a-skank.

– Even passed out the only way anyone will touch you is with a pen.

– Hashtag-Sarah-is-a-skank.

– Not so up yourself now, are you?

– That'll teach you for stealing Matt off me. Hashtag-Sarah-is-a-skank.

– You're so out of order.

– Stupid bitch.

– Why don't you just curl up and die.

– Hashtag-Sarah-is-a-skank.

– Hashtag-Sarah-is-a-skank.

– Hashtag-Sarah-is-a-skank.

– The Sarah-is-a-skank hashtag is trending.

– How funny!

– Have you seen her in school since?

– No.

– Don't blame her.

– Would you wanna face all that?

4.

The BOYS *in the changing rooms, having been caned in their football match.* JADEN*'s on his phone.*

JADEN. Have you seen this Sarah-is-a-skank hashtag? It's jokes.

SCOTT. Funnily enough, I've got more important things to be thinking about, Jaden. I can picture my dad right now. Arms crossed, looking at me like I'm… a total failure.

CALEB. No he won't.

JADEN. It's not your fault we were missing our three best players.

SCOTT. But I couldn't pull the rest of us together, could I?

CALEB. You tried your best.

SCOTT. Not good enough.

JADEN. I can't believe they've been suspended for a stupid joke.

CALEB. Not a very funny one.

SCOTT. Don't get all moral. I saw you laughing.

CALEB. No I wasn't.

SCOTT. Yes you were! Everyone was.

CALEB. Okay, maybe I was. But all the hassle she's been getting? That's not funny. That's dark.

JADEN. Everyone'll get bored soon. Move on to something else.

CALEB. Or someone else.

Beat.

SCOTT. Me probably. Being in charge of the worst football team in the last five years.

JADEN. Yeah they probably will, but so what?

Who cares? It's not a big deal.

CALEB. This is probably the first and last time I'll ever say this, but he's right.

JADEN. See.

SCOTT. Yeah well, I care.

And my dad'll care.

CALEB. If it's gonna cause you hassle, why don't you knock it on the head for a while?

SCOTT. What?

JADEN. You think he should quit?

CALEB. No. Just... I dunno. It might help you manage your workload better if you –

SCOTT. I don't have a problem managing my workload.

CALEB. O-kay.

SCOTT. It's other people who keep... messing things up for me. Like Louise.

CALEB. Right.

JADEN. Ah, mate, I meant to tell you. This is proper jokes, right. Apparently she's running for school captain.

SCOTT. What?

CALEB. Louise is?

JADEN. Yep.

SCOTT. Oh I don't believe it.

JADEN. I also heard she's the one who got them suspended.

SCOTT. Are you kidding me!

CALEB. I think he's right you know. Mike saw her with Miss Reef.

JADEN. Did you hear that? He just agreed with me twice!

SCOTT. Hmm.

JADEN. She's such a bigmouth. Tell you what would shut her up. My cock in her mouth.

SCOTT. I'll shut you up with my fist in your mouth in a minute. This is all I need.

CALEB. Why you getting so aggy?

SCOTT. First, I get a B in my coursework cos she asks to move groups. Then I get the blame for losing a match because she got our players suspended.

CALEB. No one's blaming you.

SCOTT. So imagine what it'll be like if she's school captain.

JADEN. Hell.

CALEB. It's a popularity contest. No one'll vote for her.

SCOTT. They might.

JADEN. You think?

SCOTT. Unless…

JADEN. What?

SCOTT. Unless I run against her.

5.

– Is it true?

– About Michael and –

– No!

– Well yeah that is true.

– But we're talking about –

– Scott.

– Running for school captain.

– He's gonna smash it.

– Everyone else might as well just drop out.

– Even without hearing any of his plans?

– Doesn't matter.

– He'll be amazing!

– It's a pretend role anyway.

– A figurehead.

– Representing the school.

– Exactly.

– That's why it should be someone like Scott.

– Not Louise.

– No one respects her the way they do him.

– We should ask if he needs any help with his campaign.

– Make badges or something.

– Badges?

– I dunno. Whatever.

– Just be good to help.

– You so fancy him, don't you.

– So do you!

– Who doesn't?

SCOTT *in his room doing homework as* CHARLIE *enters*.

CHARLIE. Alright, dickhead?

Silence.

What you doing?

SCOTT. English. Trying to anyway.

CHARLIE. Just go online. Someone somewhere will already have the answers.

SCOTT. I'm nearly done.

CHARLIE. Give us twenty quid and I'll check it for you.

SCOTT. You're alright.

CHARLIE. You can't risk getting another bad grade.

SCOTT. I won't.

Beat.

CHARLIE. Dad said you quit the football team.

SCOTT....

CHARLIE. Scott?

SCOTT....

CHARLIE. He's really disappointed.

SCOTT. I don't have time for it.

CHARLIE. Since when?

SCOTT. Since I've got other things to focus on.

CHARLIE. You know if you haven't got any extracurricular stuff going on, no self-respecting university will look at you.

SCOTT. I have got stuff going on.

CHARLIE. Like what?

SCOTT. ...I'm running to be school captain.

CHARLIE. Really?

SCOTT. Yeah. Why not? Don't you think I can do it?

CHARLIE. No. Yeah. I'm sure you can. Just never thought it was really your kind of thing.

SCOTT. Just yours?

CHARLIE. ...What made you decide to go for it?

SCOTT. You know that girl Louise?

CHARLIE. The one you reckon's to blame for your B?

SCOTT. She is to blame. And you know what, she's had it in for me since Year 7, when I got chosen to be form captain instead of her.

CHARLIE. Right.

SCOTT. Anyway. She's running, so I thought... I thought I'd run against her. Show her. You know. That she's not better than me at everything.

CHARLIE. Well. I'm sure this'll really prove a point.

SCOTT. Jaden and Caleb think it will.

CHARLIE. Course they do. They're bigger pussies than you are.

SCOTT. You think it's a stupid idea.

CHARLIE. I think if you really want to show her up –

SCOTT. I do.

CHARLIE. You need to do something bigger. Girls like that – they have a superiority complex.

SCOTT. What do you mean?

CHARLIE. They think they're better than everyone else. That's why she's going for it. To give weight to her sense of entitlement. You need to show her she's not better than you. That she should just shut up and know her place.

6.

– I've been sent the link.

– Forward it to me.

– Am I on there?

– Every girl in school is on there.

– But where did they get the pictures from?

– I've never shown anyone that picture.

– It's your profile pic!

– Oh yeah.

– So they've just lifted them straight off other websites then?

– Must've done.

– What does it say?

– 'Rate this girl'.

– They're giving marks out of ten.

– That is so funny!

– Based on what though?

– Looks. Obviously.

– One.

– Hideous.

– A monster.

– But everyone gets a point for existing.

– No one's just got a one though right?

– Three.

– Solidly unattractive.

– Probably overweight.

– Too tall.

– Um models are tall.

– Too short.

– Good things come in small packages.

– Six.

– Almost attractive.

– I'd take that.

– Would still be embarrassed to be seen out with her though.

– Oh.

– With good make-up and low lighting, however –

– Is do-able.

– To be fair we've probably all been a six at some point.

– Eight.

– Beautiful.

– Banging body.

– I always knew you were an eight.

– Do you think I could put it on my CV?

– Ten.

– The most beautiful girl in the world.

– Made in a lab.

– Probably not real.

– Why do you think I only got a seven?

– I think a seven's good.

– Is it my teeth?

– What?

– You know how much I hate my teeth.

– I don't think it's anything to do with your teeth.

– At least you didn't get a three.

– Neither did you.

– A four.

– No one got under that.

– Actually a couple of people did.

– Who?

– Smelly Anna.

– Fair.

– Don't say that.

– We were all thinking it.

– They just had the guts to put it out in public.

– Who else?

– Louise.

– That's harsh.

– Is it?

– Yeah.

– I'd give her an eight.

– An eight?

– She's quite fit.

– She's an idiot.

– To each their own.

– It doesn't mean anything anyway.

– You would say that, you got a ten.

– I'd be lying if I didn't say it was flattering…

– But –

– It's one person's opinion.

– It's a laugh.

– It's jokes!

– Boys being boys.

GIRLS *are brought out like at a fashion show, and rated.*

– Two: Warthog.

– Four: Virgin.

– Three: Fat bitch.

– One: Dirty bitch.

– Five: Sket.

– Two: Skank.

– Four: Slut.

– Actually.

– I don't find it very funny.

LOUISE. Did you see Sarah run out of registration this morning?

SHABS. What did they say about her?

LOUISE. A five. 'It would've been a two but everyone knows she's DTF.'

RACHEL. Poor thing.

She never asked for any of this.

LOUISE. Uh, neither did I.

SHABS. You know why you're being targeted, don't you?

LOUISE. Cos I'm butters?

RACHEL. Louise, no.

SHABS. Cos you're the only one brave enough to put your head above the parapet. You're a threat.

LOUISE. Don't be stupid.

SHABS. You are.

LOUISE. How?

RACHEL. Powerful women threaten men's masculinity.

SHABS. Did you just make that up?

RACHEL. It's true. Look at the stick Hillary Clinton got. And I read this study right…

What?

I find this stuff interesting.

LOUISE. But I don't *have* any power.

RACHEL. You have a lot of qualities that powerful women have. You're articulate.

SHABS. Intelligent. Men don't like women to be more intelligent than them.

RACHEL. Not all men.

SHABS. Whatevs.

RACHEL. You're willing to speak up. Challenge the status quo.

SHABS. You're brave!

RACHEL. And actually, you will be part of the power structure.

If you become school captain.

LOUISE. You think this is what it's about?

Me running for school captain.

SHABS. I dunno. Maybe.

LOUISE. What happens if I win?

What'll they do then?

SHABS. Maybe they'll get bored.

LOUISE. Or maybe it'll get worse.

RACHEL. You can't give in to them.

SHABS. Lou? You know you can't.

LOUISE. So what, I'm just supposed to sit here and take it?

RACHEL. Well, ignoring it might be a good tactic. It would annoy them that you're not getting upset.

LOUISE. But then they might think they'd won.

SHABS. Which they haven't.

RACHEL. Could the school get the site shut down?

LOUISE. I'm not going to Miss Reef again. No way.

SHABS. We could –

No.

LOUISE. What?

SHABS. We could set up our own site.

Beat.

LOUISE. No.

No way.

SHABS. It would let them know what it feels like.

LOUISE. It makes us just as bad as them.

SHABS. I suppose.

RACHEL So… What then?

Beat.

RACHEL. Okay. What are they trying to do with this website?

SHABS. Make us feel crap about ourselves?

RACHEL. No.

They're trying to silence us.

They think that by humiliating us about our appearance, we'll shut up.

SHABS. Makes sense.

LOUISE. So…

RACHEL. We need to show them we won't be silenced. That we're not scared.

LOUISE. That we're more than just the way we look.

SHABS. How?

LOUISE. We're organising a slut walk.

– A what walk?

– A slut walk.

– I thought that's what you said.

– What the hell is that?

– Sounds disgusting.

– A bunch of girls showing off that they're slags.

– I'm in then!

– That's not what it is.

– Doesn't that blonde bird who was married to the rapper do
  one ever year?

– Kim Kardashian?

– I love her.

– Can you believe what happened in Paris? So sad.

– No, the other one.

– Amber Rose.

– Yeah.

– I follow her.

– She's so fit.

– I don't like girls with short hair.

– As if you'd stand a chance anyway.

– She's got some interesting things to say.

– Like?

– About gender equality and… stuff.

– Sounds boring.

– I dunno.

– I think it's quite –

– Cool.

– You gonna go?

– Maybe.

– I told my mum about it and she thought it was a brilliant idea.

– My mum thought it sounded stupid.

– My dad told me he used to go on marches all the time and I could probably do with becoming a bit more politically engaged.

– My dad said over his dead body.

– Bit extreme.

– Doesn't want me walking around calling myself a slut.

– Might not look good on the UCAS form I s'pose.

– I don't think you have to dress like a slut to go on the walk.

– Well what do you wear then?

– Whatever you want.

– Cos…

– Isn't it about saying – what is a slut?

– And… we're all sluts.

– To be honest, I think Louise is making a fuss over nothing.

– The website isn't so bad.

– You're only saying that cos you got a nine!

– Am I not allowed to be a bit proud of that?

– I would be.

– Yeah I s'pose.

– Doesn't mean it's not out of order though.

– We're more than just what we look like, aren't we?

– Oh!

– I get it.

– That's the point of the march, isn't it?

– Oh yeah.

– Maybe I will go.

– I'll go if you go.

– Cool.

– Let's go then.

– I'm not so sure.

– Why not?

– I'm scared.

– About?

– What will people say?

– Look at how much hassle Louise is getting.

– I don't think I could cope with all that abuse.

– Being called –

– Manly –

– Jealous –

– Ugly –

– Lesbian.

– Because

– Because being politically engaged

– Immediately makes you unattractive to the opposite sex.

– Doesn't it?

– Does it?

– I don't want that.

– We don't want that.

– No.

– And –

– I mean –

– Can you really be arsed?

– I don't care to be honest.

– Nothing to do with me.

– I wasn't even on the website.

– And besides.

– There are more important things to get angry about.

– I stand with…

– Paris –

– Manchester –

– Syria –

– Badgers –

– And what about –

– What about women in Saudi Arabia only recently being allowed to drive?

– FGM?

– Forced marriages –

– Murder –

– Rape –

– War!

7.

JADEN. Sluts? They wish. Wouldn't touch them with yours, mate.

SCOTT. How are they being allowed to do this?

CALEB. They asked.

JADEN. What's it even about?

SCOTT. Charlie was telling me they did one like this at his university and it was like, really anti-men.

CALEB. Really?

SCOTT. Yeah. If it's just for girls, then it's obviously against men.

CALEB. That's like saying if something's aimed at BME students then it's anti-white!

JADEN. No it's not.

CALEB. I'm pretty sure it's open to everyone, why don't we just ask them?

SCOTT. Nah. I'm not actually interested.

CALEB. So ignore it then. Just like everyone ignored Rosa when she did that march about veganism.

JADEN. Though the way those chickens are treated –

SCOTT. I just think it's unfair.

If we did a march, we'd get accused of being like, prejudiced or something.

JADEN. Yeah. It's double standards. Like the way the school make us celebrate International Women's Day, but not International Men's Day.

SCOTT. That is not equality.

JADEN. Amen.

SCOTT. Can't you see? They're playing the victim! Yeah sure, sexism used to be a problem like, a hundred years ago, but not now. We're all treated the same now, so what is it they really want?

JADEN. Preferential treatment.

CALEB. Aren't they doing it because of the website?

SCOTT. Maybe they should learn how to take a joke.

CALEB. Maybe it wasn't very funny.

   You know my sister's spent all day crying about only being
   a five.

   She's in Year 7! Who thinks it's alright to rate an eleven-
   year-old girl? Or any girl?

   Beat.

JADEN. Well I thought it was jokes.

   Total legend.

   Whoever set it up that is.

   Beat.

CALEB. You have got to be kidding me.

SCOTT. What?

CALEB. Please tell me it wasn't you?

SCOTT. It wasn't!

   Not exactly.

CALEB. What does that mean?

SCOTT. Charlie organised it.

JADEN Got Fat Ollie to set it up. Remember him? He built his
   own virtual-reality headset from scrap.

SCOTT. Don't give me that look. It was funny.

CALEB. You included my sister!

SCOTT. I didn't realise Fat Ollie was gonna include every girl in
   school. It was just a joke! I was trying to teach Louise a lesson
   and get her to back off.

CALEB. Well that backfired, didn't it.

   CALEB *stalks off in disgust.*

8.

LOUISE. Rach, you got the flyers sorted yeah?

RACHEL. You reckon two hundred is enough?

SHABS. I think two hundred is pretty optimistic.

LOUISE. And I've had some ideas about placards.

What do you think?

RACHEL. 'I'm more than the contents of my bra.'

SHABS. 'My clothes are not louder than my voice.'

I don't get it.

RACHEL. Is it like, listen to what I say rather than what I look like?

LOUISE. Kinda.

SHABS. I like this one.

'I am a ten out of ten.'

LOUISE. I had some better ones but Miss Reef said the only way the school would agree to this was if we didn't use their list of banned words.

RACHEL. Do they not get the irony of that?

SHABS. Free speech. But only if it conforms to the message we'd like you to give out.

LOUISE. Yeah well, what's more important? Being able to do this or arguing over a few words?

SHABS. S'pose.

RACHEL. Did you manage to invite Sarah?

LOUISE. Uh, yeah. She… didn't want to come.

SHABS. Fair enough.

LOUISE. So, where is everyone else?

SHABS. Well…

RACHEL. I kind of think this might be it.

LOUISE. Oh.

CALEB *enters. The girls nudge each other.*

Yeah?

CALEB. Is this where you're planning for the uh, march thing.

SHABS. Maybe. Why?

What do you want?

CALEB. I'm kind of interested in –

I wondered if I could…

I dunno.

Help or something.

LOUISE. Um…

RACHEL. You do know what it's about yeah?

CALEB. Yeah.

RACHEL. Cool. We could do with some more placards –

LOUISE. The thing is though…

SHABS. You're a boy.

CALEB. I am. Yeah.

SHABS. Well…

LOUISE. Not to be out of order or anything.

SHABS. But.

LOUISE. This is about stuff you probably wouldn't understand.

CALEB. Right.

Because I'm –

LOUISE. A boy.

Yeah.

CALEB. Okay.

LOUISE. So, I think maybe, actually... You should probably just leave.

RACHEL. We could at least let him hand out flyers or something.

LOUISE. But he might put people off joining.

SHABS. Yeah.

RACHEL. Or –

It might help get other people on board?

Other boys?

LOUISE. Do we want boys here?

SHABS. No.

RACHEL. Yes.

LOUISE. Won't they... I dunno. Just try to take over?

RACHEL. No! You kind of have to... Well –

Include everyone.

In the conversation and stuff.

If you want things to change.

SHABS. Did it tell you that in another one of your studies?

RACHEL. In Sweden right, they've actually given out a copy of this book by Chimamanda Ngozi Adichie to all sixteen-year-olds – boys and girls – to try to –

SHABS. Shut up, Rachel.

CALEB. Look I don't wanna...

It's fine. If you don't want me here.

RACHEL. We didn't say that. Did we, Lou?

LOUISE. I...

SHABS. Your choice, Louise.

LOUISE....

Thanks, but –

This is for people like us.

Not you.

A disappointed CALEB *walks off. He tried.*

9.

LOUISE *and the* GIRLS *with their placards, at the protest. Despite there not being many people there, they are absolutely giving it their all, chanting their slogans, possibly even another performance of 'Oh! Bondage! Up Yours!' They are finally being heard and it is a huge moment – exactly what* LOUISE *imagined an empowered slut walk to be.*

However, as some people look on, sneering, the joy the GIRLS *initially felt begins to dissipate. They're uncomfortable and self-conscious, especially as the sneering group begins to swell in size.*

And when the group, led by SCOTT, *rush the* GIRLS *with their faces covered, carrying flour/eggs/paint – there's a moment as the girls realise what's about to happen. Practically in slow motion, the walk is ruined as the girls are pelted with things, their placards stolen and broken. The whole thing is being filmed.*

Everyone runs off except LOUISE, *covered in stuff, and* CALEB.

CALEB. Let me help.

LOUISE. I can do it.

CALEB. I know you can.

But sometimes it's nice to have help.

LOUISE. Thanks.

Beat.

CALEB. Sorry.

LOUISE. Why? You didn't throw this stuff at me.

Did you?

CALEB. No. But…

I'm just sorry it happened.

LOUISE. Does everyone in this school hate me?

CALEB. No! No way. Why would you think that?

LOUISE. I can't go online without getting called every name under the sun and now this. Doesn't suggest I'm all that popular.

CALEB. It'll blow over.

LOUISE. Reckon you can tell me when?

Cos I'm getting a bit fed up with it.

CALEB. It's probably like, I dunno. The same few people doing it all.

LOUISE. You think?

CALEB. ... Yeah.

LOUISE. It'd just be nice if –

CALEB. What?

LOUISE. ... Nothing.

CALEB. Go on.

LOUISE. It would be nice if someone stood up for me.

CALEB. Yeah.

The thing is you're not, um –

LOUISE. What?

CALEB. Okay, well. I offered to join the march, yeah. And you said no.

LOUISE. Right.

CALEB. And actually you were kind of... rude.

LOUISE. I see. So just because a girl is forthright and confident, automatically she's rude, right?

CALEB. No. You were actually rude.

It's off-putting.

Beat.

Sorry if that upsets you.

LOUISE. No it's… You're right. You're right.

I just… This is all new to me you know. I don't know what I'm doing.

CALEB. Well… I still want to help. If you'd like?

LOUISE. Thanks. I would like that.

LOUISE *heads off as* SCOTT *approaches from another direction.*

SCOTT. Where were you earlier?

CALEB. I was busy.

SCOTT. Doing what?

CALEB. Promised I'd help my mum with some stuff.

SCOTT. Like?

CALEB. You know.

Stuff.

SCOTT. Right.

So I didn't just see you with Louise then?

Helping her clean up.

That wasn't you.

CALEB. Well –

SCOTT. Well?

CALEB. Yeah.

It was.

SCOTT. Why'd you do that?

She's an idiot.

CALEB. Actually, Scott, she's not.

SCOTT. Oh my God do you fancy her?

CALEB. No.

SCOTT. She'd be punching if you two got together. Bearing in mind she's only a three.

CALEB. There you are – right there. That's why I was talking to her.

SCOTT. Cos you feel sorry for her for being so butters?

CALEB. Cos she doesn't deserve what you're doing to her!

SCOTT. Yes she does.

She needs teaching a lesson.

CALEB. You already did.

So you can leave her alone now.

SCOTT. No – she's still going on!

She – She thinks she's better than me.

Always has.

CALEB. She's just… trying to do something good.

SCOTT. At other people's expense. At my expense!

CALEB. Not everything's about you, Scott, don't you get that?

Beat.

Look.

Maybe… Maybe I shouldn't be your campaign manager any more.

SCOTT. You're choosing her over me?

CALEB. It's not…

No. I just. First the website. Now this. I don't want to be involved like this. It's… not right. And I think you know that.

SCOTT. Whatever.

Don't need you anyway.

CALEB. Okay. Well. Good luck.

CALEB *goes to shake* SCOTT*'s hand.* SCOTT *refuses.*

SCOTT. You tell that minger of a girlfriend anything, and you'll regret it.

CALEB *smiles and walks off. A moment.* SCOTT *punches a wall.*

10.

The common room.

RACHEL. Took me ages to get that stuff out my hair.

SHABS. I had three showers and could still see it.

LOUISE. I know.

RACHEL. So what we gonna do?

SHABS. I still think we could –

RACHEL. No!

SHABS. You didn't hear what I had to say.

LOUISE. We're not setting up a rival website; we're not gonna run in the changing rooms and egg everyone and we're not giving up. Alright?

SHABS. That wasn't what I was gonna say.

RACHEL. Yes it was.

SHABS. …Yeah it was.

LOUISE. Me and Caleb have been talking and –

RACHEL. Caleb?

LOUISE. Yeah.

SHABS. I thought you didn't want any boys involved?

LOUISE. Well… I was kind of wrong about that.

It's actually been really useful getting a male view of things.

SHABS. Oh yeah that's exactly what we need. A male view.

RACHEL. Go on.

LOUISE. It's like, he's got some thoughts about why the stuff we've been saying has made people angry.

SHABS. Cos they're dicks.

LOUISE. No. Well yeah. But also –

RACHEL. They feel excluded.

LOUISE. Yes!

RACHEL. And instead of seeing us talking about girls as being like, about equality – they see it as unequal cos they're used to everything being about them.

Kind of.

SHABS. Right.

RACHEL. Which I did try to say to you before.

SHABS. So what's his suggestion then?

LOUISE. It's like… Um… Okay. How do I explain it?

So with the march, yeah?

It was maybe a bit, in your face. And about one issue yeah?

SHABS. And?

LOUISE. And because we didn't invite any boys to join us –

RACHEL. They felt attacked.

LOUISE. Maybe. And not just the boys but –

Okay. I think… people felt like we were lecturing them.

SHABS. If I could roll my eyes any harder at this, I would.

LOUISE. I know, I know. It's annoying. But –

I suppose what I'm getting at, is we should try to open the conversation out more.

SHABS. How?

LOUISE. So, the main thing we're talking about is the way we're being treated as women but like, don't ignore other things.

SHABS. Like?

LOUISE. Like…

Argh this is really hard cos I don't like, totally understand it all yet but –

We have to look at how treating girls equally benefits everyone.

And how, how –

RACHEL. It's just about making sure we're being intersectional.

And yes, I did read about it.

And I did try to explain before –

LOUISE. I know, but I didn't understand then, okay?

RACHEL. And it was only talking to a boy that made you?

LOUISE. Rach…

SHABS. Just tell us what you want to do and we'll be there. Won't we, Rachel.

RACHEL. …. Yeah.

LOUISE. I want to start a group. A group that meets once a week to talk about all the things we think are unfair.

And anyone can come.

11.

During this scene, CHORUS *members begin to bleed into the real world of the play, as they take the plunge and join* LOUISE*'s group, so can be speaking from within the world, rather than sitting outside of it.*

– Did you go?

– No!

– I did.

– Me too.

– Really!

– Yeah.

– Why?

– Didn't think it was your thing.

– You said Louise was an idiot.

– Causing a fuss about nothing.

– Well –

– She is annoying.

– No denying that.

– But –

– She didn't deserve to have her walk ruined.

– I thought it was funny.

– You would.

– And all the hassle she's been getting.

– It kind of made me think –

– Maybe she's not making a fuss over nothing.

– Maybe she's got a point.

– Cos when you look at how Sarah's been treated too…

– That was all her own fault.

– Was it though?

– I spoke to my mum about it.

– My mum would go nuts if she knew any of that.

– So would my dad.

– She made me see things a bit differently.

– How?

– That maybe Louise is talking some sense.

– I still think it's ridiculous.

– She's doing it cos she's jealous of the rest of us.

– Of the male attention we get.

– I don't think so.

– The meeting's are actually… alright you know.

– You don't burn your bras then?

– Or make voodoo dolls of the boys.

– It's not about hating boys.

– So what is it about?

– Just like… Well.

– We wrote a list of all the little acts of sexism we've experienced.

– You're sixteen. How have you ever experienced sexism?

– Being called rude names when I don't give someone the attention they want.

– Mr Green only ever picking boys to answer questions in his class.

– No, he doesn't.

– He does.

– Next time you're in science I bet you'll notice.

– Rob.

– Ollie.

– Aran.

– Oh my God you are so right!

– But also the other way round too.

– How the boys get told off for hanging round the main entrance but the girls don't.

– And they're not allowed to have long hair.

– Stuff like that.

– What's the point in a list?

– Well I think we're gonna try to come up with ways of like, raising them with the school or something. See if we can make little changes.

– Cool.

– So were there many people there?

– Yeah.

– Loads of boys.

– Sean reckons it's the perfect place to pull!

– You know who else showed up?

– No.

– Sarah.

– Didn't say anything though.

– She probably needs a group like that.

– Maybe we all do.

– So –

– You think you might vote for Louise now?

– Yeah.

– When you listen to her –

– She makes sense.

– I'll vote for her if you do.

– What about Scott?

– I mean, he's fit and funny and clever and that –

– But –

– What does he actually stand for?

– What does he actually want?

12.

SCOTT *doing homework as* CHARLIE *enters*.

CHARLIE. Alright, dickhead.

SCOTT. I told you to stop calling me that.

CHARLIE. Ooh what's wrong with you? On your period?

SCOTT. Yeah.

CHARLIE. So what's with the mood?

SCOTT. Nothing.

CHARLIE. They've not managed to connect you to the website, have they?

SCOTT. No.

CHARLIE. Told you they wouldn't be able to trace it. Ollie might be a fat freak with no friends but he knows computers.

SCOTT. Yeah.

CHARLIE. He's done something with it that means it'll take ages for it to be taken down too.

SCOTT. Great.

CHARLIE. So you should start thinking what else you want to go on there. Maybe footage from the march? I can't stop watching the bit where that bitch gets hit in the face with the first egg. Ollie's made a gif I can send you.

SCOTT. No. Thanks.

I was actually kind of thinking… maybe we should just leave it now.

CHARLIE. Are you kidding me?

Everyone's talking about it. You're a total legend.

SCOTT. Some people didn't find it funny.

CHARLIE. Only people with no sense of humour.

SCOTT. Caleb.

CHARLIE. Ignore him. Me and Dad used to call him Cry-Baby Caleb when you were at Infants cos he used to cry every time his mum left him there.

　　You don't need someone like that around.

SCOTT. Nah. Yeah. S'pose not.

CHARLIE. And anyway, it did what you wanted to and shut that idiot up, didn't it.

SCOTT. Kind of.

CHARLIE. What do you mean?

SCOTT. She's still running for school captain.

CHARLIE. You'll beat her easily though.

SCOTT. I thought I could.

CHARLIE. Not any more?

SCOTT. Dunno. Like I said, some people didn't think the website and that were funny.

　　They've started this group. Meet once a week.

　　It's like a society or something.

CHARLIE. About what?

SCOTT. I'm not sure. A girls' society maybe?

CHARLIE. Yawn. Still banging the same 'inequality' drum then.

SCOTT. Yeah. Quite a lot of people have joined though.

CHARLIE. So start a rival group. A boys' society.

SCOTT. They let boys in too.

CHARLIE. How progressive. Look, just ignore them. A stupid society isn't gonna get in your way.

SCOTT. Yeah. No.

　　I dunno though.

CHARLIE. People will get bored of her ranting on about the same thing soon enough.

SCOTT. But what if they don't? What if she's got a point?

CHARLIE. She hasn't got a point. Her and her friends just keep playing the victim to get special treatment. Shouting sexism when things don't go their way.

It's ridiculous.

SCOTT. Yeah.

CHARLIE. So all we need to do is show what a bunch of hypocrites they are, and no one will listen to another word that comes out of their mouths. And you will walk this election.

13.

– The website's been updated.

– With that video from the march?

– No.

– What then?

– Have a look.

– Just tell us.

– I don't want to ruin it for you.

– Is it that good?

– They put new pictures of the girls up.

– Ooh.

– Not naked ones.

– Oh.

– And not all the girls this time.

– Just ones who joined that society.

– What does it say?

– New ratings?

– I think with this new hair I'll have gone up to a seven.

– It says –

– HYPOCRITES.

– 'Why are these slags allowed a society?'

– Then under each picture

– It outlines their sex lives.

– Seriously?

– Yep.

– Like what though?

– People they've slept with.

– Stuff they've done.

– That's mad!

– That's disgusting.

– Shouldn't do it if you don't want people knowing about it.

– It's private.

– It's nobody else's business.

– Nothing's private any more.

– I don't get it.

– Why do it?

– To embarrass them?

– Maybe.

– It's making a point.

– Which is?

– Should they be allowed this society if they're opening their legs for everyone?

– Um –

– I suppose it is quite hypocritical.

– No.

– It shows exactly why we need this society.

Common room. The CHORUS *members who became part of the society will be in this scene.*

RACHEL. My dad's gonna kill me.

SHABS. He won't find out.

RACHEL. Everyone in school's been sent the link!

SHABS. So tell him it's not true.

RACHEL. You know I can't lie.

SHABS. Well you did a pretty good job of not telling us you'd shagged Michael.

RACHEL.….I'm sorry.

SHABS. Rach, I'm winding you up.

I don't care who you sleep with.

RACHEL. Thank you.

SHABS. But Michael though, really?

Jokes. Jokes.

RACHEL. I thought he was nice.

I thought he liked me.

SHABS. So nice he's been bragging about it.

RACHEL. Not necessarily.

SHABS. How else did it get out?

RACHEL. I did think maybe it was some kind of WikiLeaks thing where our phones had all been hacked or something.

SHABS. No.

RACHEL. No.

I know.

Beat.

Shabs?

SHABS. Yeah?

RACHEL. Do you –

Do you think they're right?

SHABS. What do you mean?

RACHEL. Are we hypocrites?

For, you know.

Having sex.

SHABS. How is that hypocritical?

RACHEL. Because this all started cos Sarah was called a slut and I suppose, well –

Are we?

SHABS. No.

Beat.

RACHEL. It's so complicated, isn't it.

SHABS. Actually, it's not.

It's really simple.

We're entitled to do whatever we want with our bodies.

And no one else has the right to say anything about it.

A furious SARAH enters.

SARAH. Where is she? Where's Louise?

SHABS. …I'm not sure.

SARAH. Right. Well when you see her, tell her I'm done, okay? I never wanted any of this. I never asked for it. You know all I really wanted? I wanted to change schools. I begged my mum to let me and she said no. Told me it'd all blow over, everyone would stop talking about me when a new bit of gossip came along. Oh yeah, and she also grounded me for a month for getting so drunk, as if I needed any more punishment after…

LOUISE enters.

So I kept my head down, tried to keep going, but it hasn't blown over and you know why? Cos she hasn't let it. She just kept bringing it up, kept using my name to further some stupid cause that I'm not even interested in, and now look! Everything's got worse. And not just for me, but all of you. So thank you. Thank you for ruining my life.

SARAH rushes off.

RACHEL. Sarah!

SHABS. You gonna go after her?

LOUISE. I don't think she wants me to.

RACHEL. She's upset.

LOUISE. She's right to be.

Look what I've done to her. To all of us. I started this cos I thought she… I thought we all needed a voice. But all I've done is make things worse.

SHABS. Short term maybe. But once we get through all this –

LOUISE. What? What will actually change?

RACHEL. Louise –

LOUISE. Nothing.

I'm out.

During this next section, the CHORUS *members who joined the society are reabsorbed into the* CHORUS.

– Louise has closed the society?

– Oh.

– Wow.

– I don't blame her.

– I couldn't have put up with everything she did.

– If you're in the public eye, you've got to expect some negativity.

– All celebrities get trolled.

– Even the popular ones.

– She's not in the public eye.

– All she did was call out some sexism.

– And got a bucketload more.

– Which she didn't deserve.

– Yes she did.

– What?

– She wound people up.

– No one likes being told what they can and can't say.

– Or do.

– She looked down on us.

– Thought she was superior

– Just cos we don't mind getting whistled at.

– It was her own fault really.

– She was asking for it.

– I think it's a shame.

– I was quite enjoying those meetings.

– Me too.

– I don't think she had a choice.

– Miss Reef told her to apparently.

– Really?

– Yeah.

– That's –

– Awful.

– She gets eggs thrown at her, abused online.

– Then she's the one who's punished by having to close the
    society down?

– It was her behaviour that caused all this.

– Getting the boys suspended, the march, the society.

– It was inflammatory.

– Nah.

– There's something a bit backwards about that.

– Makes me feel a bit funny.

– Poor cow.

14.

LOUISE, *alone in her room. The light is different, eerie.*

EMMELINE. Louise?

LOUISE. Um, sorry, do I know you?

Did my mum let you in?

EMMELINE. No.

Don't you recognise me?

LOUISE. I'm really sorry but –

No.

EMMELINE. Turn to page fifty of your history textbook.

LOUISE. Oh.

You're –

EMMELINE. Emmeline Pankhurst.

Yes.

LOUISE. This is weird.

EMMELINE. I know. But do go along with it, dear.

LOUISE. Okay.

Are you –

Why are you here?

EMMELINE. I've been watching your campaign with interest, and thought you could do with some moral support.

Three more figures step forward and EMMELINE *introduces them.*

LOUISE. Um…

EMMELINE. Hillary Clinton – she's been through similar herself; Chimamanda Ngozi Adichie has some interesting thoughts on the subject; and Michelle Obama, who is just so fantastically supportive of young women like yourself I thought if anyone can gee you up – it's her.

A fourth figure appears.

MADONNA. Sorry, sorry I'm late.

MICHELLE. Pop star's prerogative.

HILLARY. Madonna? I didn't know you were invited.

EMMELINE. She is a glass-ceiling shattering, boundary-breaking, kick-arse pop star. Katy Perry, Beyoncé et al – wouldn't exist without our Madge.

MADONNA. All true. And you know me. I just love to throw my two pence into political discussions.

LOUISE. Well, no offence but you're all a bit late now.

MICHELLE. It's never too late.

LOUISE. Society's closed and there's no way I can beat Scott in the elections.

So it basically is.

Beat.

I just didn't think it would be so hard.

HILLARY. I know.

LOUISE. I don't get why it's made people so angry.

MICHELLE. Well.

The thing is, most people think the battle's been won. In the West at least.

Women have the vote.

They have access to education

Workplace equality.

EMMELINE. The UK's had two female Prime Ministers, people, isn't that evidence enough!

CHIMAMANDA. What more could they possibly want?

These women, they have it all but are still fighting.

MADONNA. Whinging.

CHIMAMANDA. And why is that?

Is it because they're still experiencing daily inequalities and prejudices due to their gender?

HILLARY. Sat at the table but being ignored and talked over?

MADONNA. Treated as nothing more than vaginas on legs?

LOUISE. I feel slightly uncomfortable with your use of the word vagina.

EMMELINE. Tough.

HILLARY. No!

It's because they don't really believe in equality.

MICHELLE. What they really want, is to be treated favourably over men.

CHIMAMANDA. To have quotas –

HILLARY. And positive discrimination –

MICHELLE. So they can have a bigger bite of the cherry.

EMMELINE. And that is why people think feminism is a dirty word.

LOUISE. Um, yeah.

Totally.

Agree with all of that.

The thing is though, I'm not a –

The stuff I've been doing.

That's not feminism.

CHIMAMANDA. So what is it then?

LOUISE. I –

I dunno.

It's just.

I just want everyone to be treated fairly.

EMMELINE. Okay.

> We're not here to lecture you.

> Feminism obviously needs a massive rebrand.

CHIMAMANDA. I am trying.

MICHELLE. We all are.

HILLARY. Did you know that Chimamanda's book about feminism has been given to all sixteen-year-olds in Sweden?

LOUISE. Oh. Yeah someone did try to tell me that.

EMMELINE. Anyway. For the sake of argument.

MICHELLE. And semantics.

EMMELINE. Take it from us.

ALL. You're a feminist.

MADONNA. And that's nothing to be ashamed of.

LOUISE. But what am I supposed to do about it?

> Everything I've tried so far hasn't worked.

> And isn't smashing windows, burning bras and pointy bras all a bit –

EMMELINE. Passé?

LOUISE. Yeah.

EMMELINE. In the face of a terrible onslaught, a very wise woman – Hillary, in fact – once said:

> 'When they go low, we go high.'

MADONNA. That would make a great song title.

HILLARY. Um actually… I was quoting Michelle.

CHIMAMANDA. Credit where's it due.

MICHELLE. Thanks, guys.

EMMELINE. Oh. Terribly sorry. But… You get my drift, yes?

LOUISE. 'When they go low, we go high.'

15.

School hall. Everyone was gathered for the school-captain announcement, and the crowd is beginning to dissipate.

CALEB. Congratulations.

SCOTT. You don't mean that.

CALEB. I do actually.

I know how much it meant to you to win.

SCOTT. My dad... He's actually proud of me. For once.

CALEB. So it was worth it then.

SCOTT....

Caleb?

Do you think...

Do you think I'd have won without all the... stuff?

CALEB....You were always gonna win.

SCOTT. Oh what cos I'm a boy?

CALEB. No. You won cos people like you. They listen to you. Always have.

And cos you're so used to it, you don't understand how powerful that is.

SCOTT *watches sadly as* CALEB *walks off*.

RACHEL. Why are we still waiting around? Is he gonna give a speech or something?

SHABS. I can't think of anything I want to do less than hear that dope boast about winning.

JADEN. You should be a bit more respectful to your new leader.

RACHEL. Or what?

SHABS. This isn't North Korea.

He's not gonna nuke us if we slag him off.

JADEN. Maybe not.

But he can make your life hell.

SHABS. Maybe this is North Korea.

– Scott won?

– Yeah. Obviously.

– I'm kind of annoyed by that.

– I'm not.

– I voted for him.

– Me too.

– I was always going to.

– After Louise shut the society it was on the cards really.

– Someone should've grassed him up for that website.

– You think?

– Yeah.

– She's still got the moral high ground.

– Which is meaningless.

– Cos what can you actually do with that?

> LOUISE *walks through the crowd to* SHABS *and* RACHEL.
> *They smile supportively at her.*

SHABS. Least you didn't come last.

LOUISE. Good old Smelly Anna.

RACHEL. You should give a speech.

LOUISE. I've had enough public humiliation to last me a
lifetime, thanks.

SHABS. Go on. There are still people interested in what you
have to say.

A reluctant LOUISE *gets up and begins to speak, initially just to* SHABS, RACHEL, CALEB *and maybe a couple more.*

LOUISE. Um, hi. I can't pretend I'm not gutted about losing, but you voted Scott to be your new school captain. He won. Fair and square. So congratulations, Scott. I hope it's worth it. I really do.

A microphone drops down from the ceiling and the lights change, with a spotlight on LOUISE. *This is her moment. During the rest of her speech, the crowd listening to her becomes larger and larger, until it's the whole company* (*barring* SCOTT *and* JADEN).

Although I'm walking away from here a loser in some people's eyes, I still feel like a winner. Cos I've learnt some really important things. I – I didn't get everything right over the past couple of months. This is all new to me and – I hope people can understand that and forgive me and see that… it all came from a good place.

It was Emmeline Pankhurst who said: 'Men make the moral code and they expect women to accept it. They have decided that it is entirely right and proper for men to fight for their liberties and their rights, but that it is not right and proper for women to fight for theirs.' A hundred years later and it feels like we've not moved forward at all.

Since the day I decided to stand for school captain, I've been put through it. Attacked online. Attacked in person. And you can all stand there and pretend it was for a million different reasons. Pretend it was my fault. I asked for it cos I'm annoying or… whatever. But deep down, we all know the only thing I did wrong was be a girl who spoke up. A girl who refused to stay silent. And even though I lost, I'm still not gonna stay silent, because this stuff is too important to keep ignoring.

Strong people don't need to put others down to make themselves feel good. Strong people lift others up. I am a strong person. And I'm gonna use that strength to keep going. To listen. To communicate. To lift others up when they're put down. And most of all, to continue to fight for my and every other woman and every other person's liberties and rights. Cos we could all do with being lifted up at the moment.

– So.

– That's our story.

– The one that started on an ordinary Saturday in September.

– Or earlier.

– Hundreds of years earlier.

– If you want to look at it in the context of something bigger.

– It might also be your story too.

– Not exactly the same.

– But –

– Maybe you've been silenced.

– Because of your gender.

– Your race.

– Age.

– Background.

– We've tried to understand why people do the things they do.

– But actually –

– What we've discovered –

– Is –

– It's really really complicated.

– Everyone has different opinions.

– Everyone uses different 'facts' to make their point.

– No one's right

– And everyone's wrong.

– But –

– If there's two things to take away from this story –

– It's –

– If you believe in something –

– Do not allow yourself to be silenced –

– And –

– When they go low…

ALL. Go high.

The End.

www.nickhernbooks.co.uk

facebook.com/nickhernbooks

twitter.com/nickhernbooks